THIS IS ME!

VOICES FROM THE UK

Edited By Briony Kearney

First published in Great Britain in 2022 by:

YoungWriters® Est. 1991

Young Writers
Remus House
Coltsfoot Drive
Peterborough
PE2 9BF
Telephone: 01733 890066
Website: www.youngwriters.co.uk

Book Design by Ashley Janson

Softback ISBN 978-1-80015-811-5

Printed and bound in the UK by BookPrintingUK
Website: www.bookprintinguk.com
YB0496I

FOREWORD

For Young Writers' latest competition This Is Me, we asked primary school pupils to look inside themselves, to think about what makes them unique, and then write a poem about it! They rose to the challenge magnificently and the result is this fantastic collection of poems in a variety of poetic styles.

Here at Young Writers our aim is to encourage creativity in children and to inspire a love of the written word, so it's great to get such an amazing response, with some absolutely fantastic poems. It's important for children to focus on and celebrate themselves and this competition allowed them to write freely and honestly, celebrating what makes them great, expressing their hopes and fears, or simply writing about their favourite things. This Is Me gave them the power of words. The result is a collection of inspirational and moving poems that also showcase their creativity and writing ability.

I'd like to congratulate all the young poets in this anthology, I hope this inspires them to continue with their creative writing.

CONTENTS

St Swithun Wells Catholic Primary School, Hunters Hill

St Vincent De Paul RC Primary School, London

Wiveliscombe Primary School, Wiveliscombe

THE POEMS

All About Me

I love adventure,
Like the feeling of sand between my toes,
And the wind in my face
As I glide through a sky of pure blue.
Sketching the world through my eyes,
Getting inspiration from a TV,
The excitement of the turn of my manga pages,
Finding out what happens,
Playing games on my phone, Nintendo and iPad,
Editing photos and videos, while animating clips,
Building in Minecraft and decorating my house in Animal Crossing.
Writing poems and stories,
And making presentations and sharing them with the class.
There is no one quite like me,
Because this is all about me!

Helen Hughes (10)
ACS Egham International School, Egham

All About Me

My name is Millie and I am ten,
I go to Blackfield Primary and I have a few good friends,
I have brown eyes and my hair is light brown too,
My personality is funny and here's what I like to do,
I like to ride my bike and also play on my phone,
But when it's time to put it away, I like to sit up in my room,
I have two brothers and a sister too,
A mum and a dad, not forgetting my cat, Cookie, he's part of the family too,
My favourite subject is art,
My teacher is Miss Millage, I think she's very smart,
This poem is about me and what I like to do,
Now let's hear all about you,
I hope you liked this poem, hope to see yours too.

Millie Mcculloch (10)
Blackfield Primary School, Blackfield

Bella's Things

Bonjour, my name is Bella,
And this is all that you need to find out about me,
I love riding horses,
And playing with them,
If you make me mad then,
I will drive you crazy,
If you don't play horses,
Then I will make you play,
Day and night,
And you can't stop me
From doing what I say,
I'm unstoppable,
And I will defeat you,
There you have it.

Bella Needham (9)
Blackfield Primary School, Blackfield

Curly Locks

I planned to sleep in drippy, wet hair,
Surprise! I'm now a grizzly bear,
Stepping in for a quick shower,
Is never really in my power,
Some days I am truly sad,
My comb is my fallen comrade,
Broken hair strands everywhere,
No hair fall is so damn rare,
Hats are my biggest foe,
Humidity - oh god, no!
Oh dear, the unbearable pain
From taming the enormous mane.

Rhianne Dean (10)
Blackfield Primary School, Blackfield

Megan

M ass galaxies emote
E ndless stories told
G rey kittens laugh
A mazing singers melodise
N umerous shows materialise.

I love my acting,
It is so enjoyable,
It has common learning,
Enjoyable, hardworking,
It is tiring, I feel happy.

Megan Dyer (10)
Blackfield Primary School, Blackfield

Luna The Wonder

This is me, Poem Country,
No one can control it without their heartbeat,
I am Luna,
No one can compete,
And no one can go against me,
So here I am, telling my little story,
Knowing one day it will be glory,
Every once in a while, I write things in my diary,
I try to not write too fast!
My writing is like a book,
Think of it as the size of a dictionary,
Like when I'm in secondary,
Will I write a book?
Maybe I will become an author,
I don't know!
I like to write things about feelings,
And sometimes write little stories,
About little creepy-crawlies.

Luna Armel-Shephard (8)
Colvestone Primary School, Hackney

Me

I may be that bright light from far away,
I may be the wind blowing an oak tree,
I may be the sweetener in your afternoon tea,
I may be something that makes you happy,
I may be the sun, shining so bright,
I may be the moon, shining at night,
I may be a spirit that floated away,
I could be a feeling you get every day,
I could be a thing that you left before night,
I could be a knight fighting for something bright,
But something I do know, is that I'm something
nice,
Not as nice as a pony, not as nice as a band,
But nice enough to make you glad.

Neriah Boakye (10)
Colvestone Primary School, Hackney

Colours

The colours that make me are blue, brown, and white,
The colours that make Neriah are brown and black,
The colours that make Delphi are brown and white,
The colours that make Aoki are black and brown,
These are our appearance colours.

The colours that make me are purple and yellow,
The colours that make Neriah are blue and orange,
The colours that make Delphi are light green and navy,
The colours that make Aoki are red and pink,
These are our personality colours.

The colours that make Year 5 are
Rainbow.

Clara Torsun-Watson (9)
Colvestone Primary School, Hackney

My Friend

My friend,
She can bend,
She sometimes lends and mends,
She is funny like a hopping bunny,
She likes runny honey,
She is similar to me but lets me be,
She is sometimes bossy,
She sometimes feels blue whenever you say,
"Shoo,"
Like I said, she is like the boss,
She is like a king,
She prances when she dances,
She is a roller girl and a Cola girl,
She skates to debate,
She leads and reads,
But she is the best friend ever.

Delphi Ward (9)
Colvestone Primary School, Hackney

Cats

Cats are sneaky,
Their cat flaps are creaky,
They like to purr and lick your hand,
Their collars are like an elastic band,
Cats like to drink milk and eat fresh fish,
People like to have a nice hot dish,
If they eat chocolate or sweets, there's a chance they might die,
I promise you, it's not a lie,
They have long whiskers with a curl on the end,
It's a bit of a bend on the end.

Margot de Rosée (9)
Colvestone Primary School, Hackney

Hats

Hats small, hats tall,
I like hats, I think they're cool,
No rats wear hats,
No hats wear rats,
Bats are sneaky,
Rats are squeaky,
They're both a bit cheeky,
So, when it comes to hats it will be tricky,
Bats don't wear hats,
If you take my hat, I'll hit you with a bat,
I got it from a wombat,
But, what about that?
Cats wear top hats.

Leonides Athanasiou (9)
Colvestone Primary School, Hackney

I Like Animals

I like animals,
I like stripy or spotty ones,
I like fluffy ones,
Ones with floppy ears and waggy tails.

I like animals,
I like ones with paws and claws,
Ones that go *clippity-clop*,
Or go *clop-clop*.

I like animals,
I like them if you can keep them in your house or not,
I like them a lot.

Freya Madell (10)
Colvestone Primary School, Hackney

Personality Cookie

A bucketful of smartness,
A dash of clumsiness,
A cup full of hyperness,
A clump of thinkability,
And finally, half a bucket of imagination.

First, slowly add in the bucket of smartness, as carefully as possible,
Next, plop in that dash of clumsiness - but don't drop it!
Quickly add in that full cup of hyperness,
Drop in that clump of thinkability,
And finally, that big half bucket of imagination,
Slowly mix together and put in the oven for an hour and a half,
There you go!
You have made a nice cookie of Louisa's personality!

Louisa Stupart (10)
Darvel Primary School, Darvel

Family And Friends

My name is Katie,
I'm kind of crazy,
I have a pony, his name is Dodi,
He is cheeky but very sneaky!
I have two best friends, Erin and Orla,
I once went to Disney World Florida,
My bedroom is messy, I have clothes that are dressy,
I have a dog, her name is Roxy,
And she loves being bossy,
My dad is old and my mum is bold,
I have two brothers, Jamie and Ryan, they are annoying!
They wake up early in the morning,
I am smart, I can also play darts,
I am a horse showjumper,
Me and Dodi go as fast as thunder.

Katie Galloway (9)
Darvel Primary School, Darvel

My Favourite Animal

I am a reptile,
But when people see me, they definitely don't smile,
I slither about very happily,
But when people notice me, they act very annoyingly,
They try to catch me,
They even try to kill me,
As a pet,
The person writing this thinks I am the best,
I am mostly laid back,
I don't normally attack,
Whereas, in the wild, I'm very different,
When it comes to hunting - I'm excellent.
What am I?

Answer: A snake.

Eilidh Thomson (9)
Darvel Primary School, Darvel

Recipe For Me

A quiet dark room,
A sprinkle of light,
0.1g of rage,
A handful of kindness,
A bucketful of clumsy,
And a portion of funniness.

Now to make,
Go into the dark room,
Get a big bowl,
Put in 0.1g of rage,
Put in a handful of kindness and mix,
Get the bucket of clumsiness,
Dig a little hole and mix,
Now sprinkle the funniness in,
And you're done.

Jacob Murray (10)
Darvel Primary School, Darvel

This Is Me

One scoop of ice cream,
A dash of silly,
A glob of fun,
Three cups of intelligence,
Two pinches of hardworking,
Ten cups of kindness.

What to do:
Put the ice cream in a pot,
Add the dash of silly,
Stir, then add the glob of fun,
Put in the three cups of intelligence,
Two pinches of hardworking,
Ten cups of kindness,
Do not forget to stir it up!

Eilidh McKinnon (10)
Darvel Primary School, Darvel

This Is Me

A cup full of kindness,
A dash of funniness,
A spoonful of talking,
Two cups of cheekiness,
A dash of hardworking,
A dollop of smartness.

Add the cup of kindness to a bowl,
Put in the dash of funniness,
Don't forget about the spoonful of talking,
Add two cups of cheekiness,
Now the dash of hardworking,
And the last thing, a dollop of smartness.

Eiledh Paton (10)
Darvel Primary School, Darvel

This Is Me

I am traumatised by spiders,
I am a brilliant rollerskater,
I am passionate about ladybugs,
I am Kaila,
I have a pest of a little brother,
I can be very shy,
I am a big Potterhead,
But I also love my bed,
Writing stories is my thing,
I am as fast as a lightning bolt,
Arts and crafts are my favourite thing to do,
This is me.

Kaila Trewern (10)
Darvel Primary School, Darvel

This Is Me

T ea is terrific
H ate spiders more than heights
I love dance, it's my passion
S picy food is my favourite

I love giraffes, they're my favourite animal
S ports are my safe zone

M aths I love
E nergetic as a rabbit, this is me.

Skye Devlin (10)
Darvel Primary School, Darvel

This Is Me

T oo tall to my friends
H ave a bad habit of biting my nails
I f you can't find me, I'm usually watching Disney
S o quick when sneaking ice cream

I am obsessed with cats
S illy but friendly

M essy but tidy
E nergetic.

Emily Worn (10)
Darvel Primary School, Darvel

This Is Me

T iny as a mouse
H olidays in England are my faves
I have two best friends, Katie and Taylor
S ometimes I'm silly

I love playing Roblox
S ometimes I feel smart

M y mum and dad are kind
E xcellent at art.

Erin Atkins (10)
Darvel Primary School, Darvel

About Me

I am a pro at rugby,
And I love my cosy, cuddly cat called Cody,
And sometimes I am a nice, kind boy,
Or bad and not kind,
I am a very loyal friend,
And a good friend,
I am sometimes annoying,
And I am good at flips on the trampoline.

David Richmond (10)
Darvel Primary School, Darvel

This Is Me

T asty chicken
H ave good friends
I am as fast as a Bugatti
S mart

I like karate
S ometimes I am tired

M y room is messy
E very day.

Jamie Thomson (10)
Darvel Primary School, Darvel

This Is Me

I love football so much,
And I am great at football,
I like basketball, sometimes too much,
I am a cheeky boy,
I am a funky Fortnite freak,
Spaghetti bolognese is tasty,
Mr Bean is funny.

Aron Joyce (10)
Darvel Primary School, Darvel

This Is Me

S uper arty
A bsolutely hyper all the time
S uper sassy
S uper dancer in my bedroom
Y ellow is my favourite colour.

Courtney Stephenson (10)
Darvel Primary School, Darvel

All About Zooming Zoha

Z ooming through the playground
O h, amazing art and beautiful crafts
H elpful at home and happy
A mazing beautiful brown eyes

F antastic fashion and kind
A nnoying autumn is not my favourite season
T errific tennis, I don't like that much
I ncredible dance moves, I love to dance
M arvellous mangoes are one of my favourite fruits
A mazing athletic skills
H appy home with my loving family.

Zoha Chaudhary (9)
Mount Florida Primary School, Mount Florida

Clever Christopher

C reative Christopher
H appy Christopher has outstanding auburn hair
R eally awesome reader
I play football, I'm good in goal
S ip, sip, juice is not for me
T errific at target practice
O verjoyed me
P owerful polar bears, they are my favourite animals
H umorous Christopher
E at, eat, I love to eat
R igid rugby player.

Christopher Jobling (9)
Mount Florida Primary School, Mount Florida

All About Terrific Tola

T errific Tola is in the terrific Turtles
O la is my mum and she owns the flat we live in
L ong, large fish tank with lovely fish
A nd Tola loves animals

Z ooming Tola zooms through her house
O bsessed with animals
S hiny silver fish
I ncredible family
A rtful Tola does amazing art.

Tola Czernecka (9)
Mount Florida Primary School, Mount Florida

Super-Duper Spencer

S tupendous super Spencer
P hew! He runs like a pocket rocket
E at, eat, eat, I love to eat
N earby his friends call him
C ool weather I love in cold December
E nd of school is the best part of the day
R unning in my red trousers is really fun.

Spencer Stewart (9)
Mount Florida Primary School, Mount Florida

Willow's Wonderful World

W onderful Willow loves water
I ndependent Willow went to the park
L ovely Willow likes lollies and little cats
L ittle Willow loves her light blue eyes
O utstanding Willow likes to play outside on swings
W onderful willow trees when I walk outside.

Willow Goold (8)
Mount Florida Primary School, Mount Florida

Hyper Harris

H ungry Harris has an appetite
A mazing Harris has his blue eyes
R unning Harris was blazing down the street
R ed is my favourite colour
I ndependent Harris worked hard
S uper Harris likes bikes.

Harris Corbett (9)
Mount Florida Primary School, Mount Florida

Happy Haniah

H appy Haniah loves hot holidays
A mazing Haniah loves apples
N avy and light pink are her favourite colours
I love vanilla ice cream
A rty Haniah does amazing art
H aniah has beautiful eyes.

Haniah Jabeen (9)
Mount Florida Primary School, Mount Florida

Optimistic Oskar

O verjoyed, outstanding, optimistic blue eyes
S uper running, like a sliding snake
K nowing what to do when the teacher says
A fan of an alien and aiming to learn about aliens
R eally tries his hardest.

Oskar Jagowski (9)
Mount Florida Primary School, Mount Florida

Magnificent Maryam

M agnificent Maryam is merry
A mazing Maryam is good at art
R ed and purple are my favourite colours
Y oung Maryam is eight years old
A mazing Maryam likes apples
M arvellous Maryam is merry.

Maryam Hamid (8)
Mount Florida Primary School, Mount Florida

All About Hannah

H appy hilarious Hannah had a hamburger
A dorable adventurous Hannah had an apple
N atural green eyes sparkle in the sun
N ervous and noble
A mazing and athletic
H amster called Apple.

Hannah Mcmillan (9)
Mount Florida Primary School, Mount Florida

Joyful Joanna

J oyful Joanna likes to jump on her trampoline
O n weekdays, I do tae kwon do
A pples are my favourite fruit
N oodles are delicious
N ine years old now
A rty Joanna loves to draw.

Joanna Kozinska (9)
Mount Florida Primary School, Mount Florida

Confident Corrah

C onfident, cool Corrah
O utstanding bright blonde hair
R esponsible, ready, reading Corrah
R eally ready to learn
A mazing, athletic, active Corrah
H appy, helpful Corrah.

Corrah Campbell (8)
Mount Florida Primary School, Mount Florida

All About Dangerous Dexter

D elightful Dexter
E xcellent Dexter
e **X** tremely cool and popular Dexter
T errific and tremendous Dexter
E xtraordinary and excited Dexter
R uns like a pocket rocket.

Dexter Logan (9)
Mount Florida Primary School, Mount Florida

Cheerful Casey

C heerful Casey likes to climb cherry trees
A pples are one of my favourite fruits
S and is soft in terrific Tenerife
E ggs are gross for me
Y eet is my favourite word.

Casey Hutchinson (9)
Mount Florida Primary School, Mount Florida

Delightful Daniel

D ramatic Daniel
A mazing at guitar
N atural at parkour
I am the Flash because I am fast
E xcellent at skateboarding
L ovely, luscious hair.

Daniel Bentley (9)
Mount Florida Primary School, Mount Florida

Crazy Carter Is Caring

C onfident Carter
A ngry sometimes
R eally good at drawing
T errific at football
E lectric scooter is so much fun
R espectful to my dog, Ted.

Carter Short (9)
Mount Florida Primary School, Mount Florida

All About Marvellous Milly

M arvellous Milly mounts a mini pony
I like Irn Bru ice cream
L ikes listening to lovely lyrics
L ittle light brown hair
Y ellow yummy banana yoghurt.

Milly Grant (9)
Mount Florida Primary School, Mount Florida

Kind Katie

K nowledgable, kind Katie
A ffectionate, admirable Otto
T errific maker of tender chicken
I ntelligent, incredible dog owner
E xcellent eater of eggs.

Katie Connelly (9)
Mount Florida Primary School, Mount Florida

Jazzy Joyful Jade

J umpy Jade is like jelly
A rty Jade likes animals
D ancing Jade does dazzling dances
E xcellent Jade loves the Earth.

Jade Bonner (9)
Mount Florida Primary School, Mount Florida

All About Joyful Jonah

J elly Jonah loves to jump
O ptimistic and cheerful
N ormal and nice
A wesome somebody
H appy smiley face.

Jonah (9)
Mount Florida Primary School, Mount Florida

Lovely Leah

L eah loves her mum and dad
E xcellent at art
A mazing apples, my favourite fruit
H elpful Leah is kind.

Leah Cummiskey (9)
Mount Florida Primary School, Mount Florida

Loud Luke

L oud
U nderstanding and listens to his friends
K ind to his family
E xcellent at basketball.

Luke Bell (9)
Mount Florida Primary School, Mount Florida

All About Excellent Ella

E xcellent Ella
L aughing Ella
L oving Ella
A mazing animal lover Ella.

Ella Fitzgerald (9)
Mount Florida Primary School, Mount Florida

This Is Megan

I am a gymnast and a swimmer too,
I am a monster Lego builder,
I am weird and funny too,
I am a sister to a younger brother,
I am an owner of two guinea pigs,
My favourite colours are orange, really light blue, and violet,
My eyes are as blue as the seas and oceans.

Megan Sattar (9)
Norden Community Primary School, Norden

Ella Butler-Miller

I am a lover of McDonald's and ice cream,
I am really easy to make laugh and I love teddies,
I am as small as a mouse,
I am an animal lover, guinea pigs are my favourite,
My hair is as bright as the sun,
My favourite colour is bright, happy, yellow,
This is me!

Ella Butler- Miller (9)
Norden Community Primary School, Norden

This Is Me

T alk a lot
H ave hazel eyes
I am a loving big sister
S hih-Tzus are my favourite dog

I have blonde hair
S ometimes get angry

M y favourite animals are robins and dolphins
E very day I laugh.

Ella-Jaye Garner (10)
Norden Community Primary School, Norden

This Is Me

I am a lover of giraffes and cats,
I am a lover of doing drawing and painting,
I am proud to be a Muslim,
I am an amazing big sister,
I am a friend of giraffes and cats,
My ginger and white cat is my best friend,
My favourite cat is a ginger and white cat.

Zoya Azam (9)
Norden Community Primary School, Norden

This Is Me, The Gamer

I am a pro at Minecraft,
I am a wrestler on Gang Beasts,
I am a racer on Forza Horizon 4,
I am a lover of memes,
I am a sweat at Fortnite,
My eyes are brown marbles,
My hair is as brown as a tree trunk,
This is me!

Reuben Windsor-Welsh (9)
Norden Community Primary School, Norden

All About Me

I am a good friend,
I am a gamer,
I am sometimes crazy,
I am an animal lover,
I am sometimes silly,
My eyes are as blue as the sky,
My hair is as brown as milk chocolate,
This is me.

Ava Cotterill (9)
Norden Community Primary School, Norden

This Is Me

I am a great gamer,
I am a good swimmer,
I am sensible,
I am good at writing stories,
My favourite food is pizza,
My favourite thing to do is play video games with my friends,
This is me!

Rupert White (9)
Norden Community Primary School, Norden

Who I Am

I am a king middle fielder,
I am a pro Minecraft player,
I am as tall as a giraffe,
I am a good artist,
I am a biker,
My hair is really dark brown,
My eyes are the same colour as my hair.

Ayra Sulman (9)

Norden Community Primary School, Norden

This Is Me

I am strong,
I am fast,
I am a cat lover,
I am my cat's best friend,
I am good at art,
My favourite animals are cats and giraffes,
My favourite teddy is Buttons,
This is me.

Alayna Shafi (9)
Norden Community Primary School, Norden

This Is Me

L ucy is good at maths and art
U nderstand all things, except not good things
C amping is fun in the woods
Y oyos are fun to do tricks

L ucy loves every sport in the world
O range balls are like basketballs
V ery good at maths
E ggs I hate
S o much

F ootball is the best sport, and basketball
O ctopuses are really weird, I don't like them
O ranges are disgusting to eat
T rampolining is fun to front flip and jump high
B asketball is good and fun
A ll sports are fun, active, and you get strength
L ego is fun to build, walls, cars, and boats
L ions and tigers are cool at showing their claws
and roaring.

Lucy Cobden (9)
Priory Primary School, Bicknacre

A Poem About Me

I nspired by Emma Watson, Daniel Radcliffe and
Rupert Grint - wow
S apphire-blue eyes
A s warm as the sun
B eautiful blonde hair
E xquisite and thoughtful
L oves Harry Potter
L oves books
A s sweet as sugar and everything nice

R oblox time is the best
O f course, I love guinea pigs and dogs
S isters forever
E ducation is the best

A s pure as a melody
N ow I love playing the keyboard
N anna and Grandad are the best

J ust a sip of tea and I need biscuits
E verything I do, I love
F un, fun, fun
F rench bulldogs I love
E xtremely kind and lovely
R eally funny
Y ou now know a lot about me.

Isabella Jeffery
Priory Primary School, Bicknacre

Me

A group, special like stars,
A group that made me,
Who I am to be,
They're my family,
Rachel, Ross, Phoebe, Monica, Chandler, Joey,
And how could I forget, Jess and Charlotte too,
They each had their story,
And shared it with me.

Summer is a time for drinking milk from coconuts,
And swimming in the ocean,
And it gives me quite good motion,
So I love it,
Festive lights, Christmas snow, chocolate, sweets,
And mistletoe, this is not a time for me,
It is for family.

Woody, Buster, Bluey,
Bambi, Ernie, Tilly,
Your furry fur, your big brown eyes,
Your long sharp claws,
And, of course, your wonderful loving nature.

Willow Amelia Newman (10)
Priory Primary School, Bicknacre

This Is Me

T his is me, my eyes are as blue as the sea and I
like learning new things
H istory, baking, and being active are what I love
to do all day
I love cats and I love it when they *purr-purr-purr!*
S ensible, caring, confident, and kind I am

I love being arty and creative, I love to draw and
paint
S mart I am because I love to write and read, I
am resilient and adventurous too

M ental maths, amazing animals, confident and
creative, I love reading books, especially
adventure ones
E veryone I love and know keeps me happy, when
I'm sad I love the colour blue, and all I have left
to say is... this is me!

Lucy Machin (9)
Priory Primary School, Bicknacre

Me

I am Tenniel and I love my dog,
I sometimes interrogate with my parents,
But if I hurt my sister, well, I'll never,
She is a very good predator,
That will scare me to death!
Don't hurt my dog,
Because his bite will give you a fright,
So I've taught you a lesson,
Now pay me back with a boxing lesson,
Hold on! I haven't finished,
There is a penalty,
So that means more football time,
But no party voice,
It's only about me,
So I was in defence and number seven came,
But with my strength, I blocked it,
And other blasting territory,
See ya!

Tenniel Hawes (7)
Priory Primary School, Bicknacre

This Is Me

Bike riding is my passion
My will is strong
But fixing chains is a pain
Oily hands like greasy pans
Unable to hold the handlebars
I still prefer them to cars
Olly, flipping, falling, persevering, riding my skateboard
Driving fast, crashing hard
Driving even faster
Pepperoni, Margherita, pizza is all I eat
But pineapple is disgusting
Sausages you cannot beat
Kicking, tackling, running, scrumming
Getting tries
Face covered in mud, no need for ties
The limit is the skies
I'm tall, not small, the court I rule
I like basketball
I am cool!

Oliver Crickmore (10)
Priory Primary School, Bicknacre

All About Me

My passion is art, sketching and drawing,
Holding a pencil and creating wonders,
Colouring in, making it amazing.

Furry creatures with tails and paws,
Playing fetch at the park and tug-of-war,
Doing tricks like sit, lay down, and paw.

Holding controllers and clicking buttons,
Minecraft and Roblox are what I like to play,
I could play them all night and play them all day.

Chilling in tracksuits and watching TV,
One of my fav' things to do is watch movies,
Social media is great and I love it too,
Snapchat, TikTok, Instagram and YouTube.

Tegan Jane Williams (10)
Priory Primary School, Bicknacre

Me And My Dog

My dog likes bogs and I like frogs and dogs,
I love my dog and my frog,
When my dog sees my frog, he says, "*Woof! Woof!*"
When my frog sees his food, he thinks it's alive,
When my frog sees my dog, it tries to hide,
And he says, "Get off my land!"
When my dog sees a bog, he says to the frog,
"There is a bog," and he jumps into it,
When I come through the door,
My dog says, "*Woof! Woof!*"
And the frog says, "*Ribbit! Ribbit!*"
My frog liked my dog because he said thank you.

Elijah Cooke (7)
Priory Primary School, Bicknacre

Crocodile

C rows are the worst but crocodiles are the best
R ollies should not be made out of crocodile skin
O ctopuses don't have bones, unlike crocodiles
C oconuts don't eat crocodiles
O ctopuses are slimy but crocodiles are rough
D inosaurs are role models for crocodiles
I am a crocodile lover, bigger than anyone
L oads of people don't like crocodiles but I do
E ric is a crocodile rider
S ome people like crocodiles but I like them most.

Brodie Hall (7)
Priory Primary School, Bicknacre

This Is Me

Basketball, I'm really small
Football, I'm unstoppable
Having Dr. Pepper makes me go insane
Gonna be a pro-footballer, get out of my way
Friends and family by my side

Football I really love
Sports, that's my passion
I never knew what I could be
Friends and family made me see

Ruff, ruff, ruff
My dog, Poppy, is extremely soft
Playful but crazy
We have so many memories that I'll never forget
It's me and Poppy
Forever and ever.

Emma Johnson (10)
Priory Primary School, Bicknacre

Broken Bone

B roke, ouch, ouch. I'm in pain, I think I've broken my femur
R ide my bike, then I fell and broke my femur
O ops, I fell on my leg and I looked at an x-ray and it was my femur
K ick the ball in the goal and hit the keeper's leg and broke his femur
E ven I tried to be careful to not break my bone but I had no luck
N o other breaks

B ang! I fell off a skateboard and broke my femur
O h no
N ice doctor
E nd of another break.

Ethan Hough (7)
Priory Primary School, Bicknacre

All About Me

My passion is gymnastics,
As it's super fun to master every move
That anyone has ever done,
Dogs are great, they're like a human on four legs,
A best friend that always will play fetch,
My family is exquisite,
We all work together like fab friends forever,
I love listening to music and singing along to it too,
It turns my frown upside down,
And stops me feeling blue,
I think lollies are spectacular,
When the juicy, sweet taste hits my mouth,
My head fills up with joy.

Lois Amelia Barnard (10)
Priory Primary School, Bicknacre

I Love Mystery

M e and you, working out a mystery
Y ou and me, happy after working
S weaty and hot like a pot
T o be fun, I love it with Mum
E at lots of sweets to solve it
R apidly hard, I just want to laugh
Y ou and me, just you and me

I t is hardcore with two people
S o I want to giggle

F ree to play, don't have to pay
U nderground and I want to bounce
N ot boring, it's fun.

Rowan Lewer (7)
Priory Primary School, Bicknacre

This Is Me

I despise the fruity, yellow mould on pizza,
With an unbreaking passion,
My aqua-blue eyes staring into the light,
My blue eyes staring into the starry night,
Fantastic family,
Arsenal are my team,
Tottenham are not the dream,
Tottenham are not the team,
I don't dream for them,
Video games are one of my concerns,
They are very important to me,
I like them 'cause they keep me entertained,
And, for the last time,
Tottenham are the worst.

Edward Lavender (10)
Priory Primary School, Bicknacre

This Is Me

North London is red and no one can argue,
The Emirates emerald-green grass beams into your eyes,
In the spectacular stadium, fans hug, scream and party all night,
The atmosphere is breathtaking,
Spurs fans sit and rage and despise their team,
My family loves and supports me,
Arsenal are my team, I love and support them,
Dambury and Bicknacre I love and try and help them,
Football is my red-hot passion,
My goal is to become a footballer.

Daniel Christmas (10)
Priory Primary School, Bicknacre

The Colours Of Me

I have a very strong passion for fashion,
I always try to be me,
So just let me be,
My family, I love,
They always let me spread my wings like a dove,
I love to express myself through art,
I love every part,
My friends are the best,
If I was ill, they would never rest,
Home is the place to be,
No one can take it from me,
I love my family,
Listening to the beat,
I'm jumping around in my seat,
This is me.

Emily Axcell (11)
Priory Primary School, Bicknacre

This Is Me

This is me,
I have blue eyes,
And my brother says, I look better with a tie,
But I definitely don't agree.

I have nice neighbours next door,
They always care,
And play games fair,
Because of that, I want to play more.

My best friend is Steven,
We like to play video games,
And have lots of fun.

When we were seven,
We liked to pretend we had lots of fame,
And we liked to do it in the sun.

Motiejus Norkus (9)
Priory Primary School, Bicknacre

Me And My Pony

T his is me, Freya Cooke,
H orses and ponies are my favourite things
I think they jump really high
S ometimes I think they fly

I hate brushing off the horse stains, it drives me insane
S illy is what my horse is made of, even though he's sweet as pie

M arvellous horses and ponies are the best, not pests
E ating treats are what me and my pony are all about, munch, munch!

Freya Cooke (9)

Priory Primary School, Bicknacre

Me And My Dog's Life

M y dog
E ats with me

A s he loves me, I love him
N ow he gives me cuddles
D ogs are fun

M y dog likes playing
Y ummy, he barks

D one, he barks
O h, there's no more
G ood, I say
'S illy dog

L ife is important to my dog
I love my dog
F inished, he says
E at, he barks.

Harry Morrish (7)
Priory Primary School, Bicknacre

World Wrestling Entertainment

W WE
O bviously, I love WWE
R aw is the best
L ovely Smackdown
D rew McIntyre claymored Big Show, he was brave

W WE Champion is Big E
W restling is amazing
E ntertainment

I t is great, Samoa Joe KO punched Finn Balor

L et me wrestle The Rock
O wen loves WWE
V ery good
E very time it is on, I watch it.

Owen Black (7)
Priory Primary School, Bicknacre

Marvellous Me

We are independent and free,
We are all unique,
We are all undefeated,
Be creative like marvellous me,

We can do anything, see,
Don't ever shriek,
My favourite game is hide-and-seek,
Be special, like marvellous me,

I love to go on holiday,
I hate to go to bed,
One very annoying brother,

My favourite day is Sunday,
My least favourite word is dread,
I like my mother.

Alex Almond (10)
Priory Primary School, Bicknacre

This Is Me

Spanners, screwdrivers and hammers make my day
Fixing lawnmowers
Hip hip hooray!
Old clothes getting grubby
Washing my hands in water warm and bubbly
Caring for loved ones
I don't want to lose one
Grandad teaching me all about the wars
No time for the bores
So many dream cars I cannot choose
Only one I'll be able to use
Ferrari F40 or a Dodge
Which one shall I drive past the lodge?

Finley Roberts (10)
Priory Primary School, Bicknacre

All About Me

This is Charlotte,
The crazy banana thing,
I am a creative work of art,
Which fills my blank paper,
My paintbrush is my magic wand,
Mickey Mouse is my friendly dude,
And also I love sugary food,
Disney films are my fave,
Yorkshire puddings I crave,
Friends are by my side every day,
I hope they always stay,
Forever in my heart,
BTW, I still love art,
This is me, the Friends lover!

Charlotte Cook (10)
Priory Primary School, Bicknacre

My Mind

With the sweet sparkle in your eyes,
The touch of your fingers,
You take my breath away,
I think that, if you were gone,
There would be a huge hole in my life,
You are the shining light in my life,
The words flowing away from your imagination,
It transfers you into another world,
The melody brings you alive,
The sweet sugar fills your mouth with wonder,
It's like a fountain full of joy.

Karmann Black (10)
Priory Primary School, Bicknacre

This Is Me

From the point of view of a cat

I am a cat.
I am in love with a dog.
I love to steal dog food all the time.
Day and night!

I am soft.
I am fluffy.
I love to lay in the middle of a soft sofa, a warm bed and a homemade chair bed.
I am lazy!

I am a cat.
I trust you if you stroke my belly.
I love it when you stroke my nose.
I have a happy life and...
I love Kayleigh!

Kayleigh Valentine (8)
Priory Primary School, Bicknacre

Me

This is me,
Synchronised swimming is fun, *splash!*
I'm very clumsy - *smash!*
I love to drink tea.

I'm a cheerleader,
I love skiing,
I also love to bake,
I am an excellent reader.

I love ghosts,
My favourite colour is blue,
Like the sky,
Marmots are adorable.

I love eating roasts,
I love eating pie,
Roblox is enjoyable.

Eliza Crickmore
Priory Primary School, Bicknacre

My Dog Frankie And My Switch

F rankie is good, Splatoon 2 is good too
R onnie I wanted to call her, my silly dog Frankie
A lso, she puts her head in a water barrel
N aughty Nintendo keeps on making me download games
K angaroo Frankie, really jumpy Frankie is
I am good at playing games on the Switch, every game I am good at
E very game Frankie likes, as well as eating, she really does!

Daniel Sheriff (7)
Priory Primary School, Bicknacre

Harry's Life

You will need:
One Ryzen CPU,
One Nvidia 3080 graphics card,
Two 16TB SSDs,
One Mrs Chandler,
One Mrs Thompson,
Ten Diet Cokes,
Thirty cakes,
Ten teaspoons of happiness,
Twenty spoons of sugar.

Now get the ingredients and mix,
Heat the oven to 180 degrees,
Then put the mix into the oven for thirty minutes,
Then you have got Harry!
Have fun!

Harry Castle (7)
Priory Primary School, Bicknacre

This Is Me

The passion of the beautiful game brings us together,
To be honest, it keeps me afloat on a blue diamond sea,
We've got a brilliant defensive duo,
We've also got master midfielders that could end a move,
Or pick out a world-class pass,
Now let's talk about fabulous attack,
Goals, goals, goals and more,
Then you've got your explosive wingers who shush the crowd.

Oliver James Curtis (10)
Priory Primary School, Bicknacre

My Favourites

Manchester City, Ipswich, Nottingham Forest,
The reds are great,
The citizens are better,
Ipswich all the way in League One,
Football brings everyone to life,
McDonald's with the drip of ketchup, as I bite into my favourite food,
Gaming is one of my favourites too,
BMX-ing in video games,
BMX-ing in real life,
Both are as fun as each other!

Rory O'Connell (10)
Priory Primary School, Bicknacre

I Love Ponies

P osh, like show ponies, they are very posh
O bsessed with ponies because most of my family has one
N ice, beautiful, kind little ponies, my pony is called Ocean
I like the ocean, when I say Ocean, I think of the ocean
E ating, horses eating grass in the field, I love the sound of horses eating grass
S mart-looking pony, Ocean.

Francesca Stacey (9)
Priory Primary School, Bicknacre

All About Me

PS4 is my favourite thing,
Dogs are so cute, I love them too,
Basketball is my favourite sport,
Shooting ball, I always score,
I help my mum clean all day,
After that, I play and play,
Roblox time, yay, yay, yay!
Art is my thing,
Playing in the waves,
Feet in the sand,
Nice on my skin,
Burgers after the beach,
Yum, yum, yum.

Mya Colquhoune (9)
Priory Primary School, Bicknacre

My World

I love my funny, quirky family so much,
They really are a funny bunch,
Luna is my little kitty,
She is very, very pretty,
I'm as happy as can be,
With musical notes dancing around me,
When I put my headphones on,
I bounce my head to the beat of the song,
I love hearing the waves crash against the rocks,
Even though I get wet socks!

Rachel Archer (10)
Priory Primary School, Bicknacre

My Favourite Things To Do

Hiss! My bike tyre is going down,
I hope I don't fall to the ground,
My bike has ten gears,
And I don't like the taste of beer,
I like gardening,
But certainly not barking,
Fantastic football, flying through the air,
I hope we don't need a flare,
My terrific tablet, oh so fun,
Playing Roblox while eating a bun.

Isaac Arden (10)
Priory Primary School, Bicknacre

This Is Me

I love playing for D&B,
Although it won't stay with me,
I love my house,
It's lovely,
They wear the kit in red and white,
I watch them play every night,
My friends and family are so lovely,
They always look after me,
I play with them every day,
Never mind Arsenal,
I'm playing all day,
All about me.

Leo Black (10)
Priory Primary School, Bicknacre

Friends

F amily is the best thing ever
R unning is my favourite sport
I am as nice as pie and as sweet as sugar
E ating pancakes is a special delight
N ice and kind, try my best to be the best
D inosaurs are really cool and they are my favourite
S mart and know many times tables and am good at English.

Ross Lowe (9)
Priory Primary School, Bicknacre

My Friends And Me

I like doing jumps on my bike,
And doing stunts on my scooter,
Spending time with my friends,
Sometimes I get upset when I fall off my bike,
But now I am getting used to it,
This is me.

I help my teacher,
I am popular in my class,
I would stick up for my friends,
I would fight for my friends,
This is me.

Ronnie Mallon (9)
Priory Primary School, Bicknacre

My Family

Me and my dad ride our bikes
On the road on Saturdays,
Cars go by,
I am scared but my dad says,
"Don't be scared, I am here."
I say, "Okay,"
But I'm still scared,
"Let's go home and pick up Mum."
When we picked Mum up,
We went straight home and relaxed,
And watched TV.

Craig Belton (8)
Priory Primary School, Bicknacre

All About Me

Dance is my passion - I love how the music flows through my body.
Music is what I love the most - it entertains me whenever I'm bored.
Gymnastics is my favourite - there are lots of tricks, I want to get better and better.
Reading is great - it calms me down and I can escape to another world.
These things make my heart full of joy!

Rosie Ward (8)
Priory Primary School, Bicknacre

This Is Me

Hi, I'm Sophie,
And I love school,
My best friend Karmann helping me all the way,
When I go home,
I see my joyful cats waiting at the doorstep,
I skip up the stairs,
To see Eva playing with all my toys,
I jump on my bed and start thinking,
I can't wait to go horseriding at the weekend,
This is me!

Sophie Willmott (11)
Priory Primary School, Bicknacre

My Dog Maddie

Maddie is my beloved, beautiful dog,
She sleeps on my bed every night, day, 24/7,
She snuggles with my toys,
She plays crazily,
She turns my frown upside down,
She makes my day,
She makes me laugh,
She loves belly rubs,
She barks at the doorbell,
Naughty!
She licks you until you can't take it.

Rafael Barbosa (8)
Priory Primary School, Bicknacre

Oscar

O h, how I love star-spotting
S tar Wars is the best
C ars are cool
A nd I love the RAF
R eading is amazing
'S eeing friends is so fun

B iking is my favourite
I am doing a test
K icking a ball is cool
E ating cake is the best

Oscar Davis (9)
Priory Primary School, Bicknacre

All About Me

Lightning fast, up and down at hypersonic speed I go,
Marble yellow ball, getting hit back and forth,
And I go for the fantastic winner,
Beeb! Borb! Bang! As I win,
Sugary sweets make me bounce off the walls,
That brownish colour melting in your mouth,
The solid ball got caught in my soft palms.

Daniel Panayiolides (10)
Priory Primary School, Bicknacre

The Great Poem

T oday is fun because we are doing poems
H ot day it is today
I ndoors is boring but outdoors is fun
S ausages are yummy in my tummy

I gloos are fun and very cool
S unny days are fun

M aking stuff is cool
E lephants are colossal giants.

Jude King (7)
Priory Primary School, Bicknacre

Out Of My Heart

With all my heart,
All my music,
All my love,
Every step I take,
I make,
With my heart,
Without taking it apart,
I love it,
With the movement,
Having a little dance,
When you put one foot in front of another,
And doing it together,
With the adventure,
This is me.

Sadie Stevens (8)
Priory Primary School, Bicknacre

Land Rover

L and Rover is my life
A nytime or anywhere
N othing beats the Land Rover
D iscovery 2 is the best

R evving the engine
O ff-roading in the Land Rover
V ery exciting and loud
E xhilarating
R ear suspension to get up hills.

Samuel Rosam (9)
Priory Primary School, Bicknacre

This Is Me

I love dogs, also sloths,
Art is my thing,
And I like swings,
Waffles and pancakes,
Pizza and burgers,
They're all my favourite foods,
My best friend loves Fidget and me too,
My favourite subjects are art and PE,
And English too,
Maths is okay,
But sport is great!

Annabel Chambers (9)
Priory Primary School, Bicknacre

How Much I Love WWE

Wrestling is so fun!
My favourite one is Stone Cold Steve Austin,
My favourite kind of matches
Are the 'Hell in a Cell' and 'TLC' ones,
I also like Rey Mysterio, The Rock,
The Viper, The Apex Predator,
Randy Orton, the phenomenal AJ Styles!
I wish I was a wrestler.

Cameron O'Riordan-Branch (7)
Priory Primary School, Bicknacre

I Love Football

I love football,
I think it's cool.
At home on the pitch,
What way will I switch?
My position is right-back,
No time to slack.
My friends, my team,
We work like a dream.
One day on TV,
At the World Cup you will see me!

This is me!

Harry Stapleton
Priory Primary School, Bicknacre

The Pizza Poem

I love cats and watching TV all the time,
I also love playing video games,
I love music,
And playing the ukulele and electric guitar,
I really love pizza,
And I also love guinea pigs, rabbits and chinchillas,
And I love sleeping on the weekend,
This is me.

Heath Huggett (8)
Priory Primary School, Bicknacre

The Recipe Of Me

Four teaspoons of investigating,
One thousand books,
Ten thousand numbers,
And a mouthful of happiness,
I have got two hundred teaspoons of space,
You have got to have 101 pounds of reading and learning,
And stir it all together,
And you will find me.

Henry Cogan (7)
Priory Primary School, Bicknacre

Me

My hungry ball of fur is the best pet of all,
The jade steamy loco is very tall,
My loving family has a lot of stuff,
My teddies are covered in a lot of fluff,
And last of all is my piece of digital fun,
That is my PlayStation which is near my toy gun.

Oliver Stephen Gaynham (10)
Priory Primary School, Bicknacre

All About Me

When I wake up in the morning,
I feel right as rain,
Every day, my brother drives me insane,
Everyone said,
My brilliant baking deserves five stars,
I always put my candy bars in my favourite jar,
And my popping candy goes, *pop-pop-pop*.

Hollie-Mae Blanchard (10)
Priory Primary School, Bicknacre

This Is Me

T igers are my favourite animal
H orse lover and rider
I am silly
S illy songs

I am silly
S ad sometimes

M y pony is my favourite
E ating is healthy and it is good for me.

Millie John (8)
Priory Primary School, Bicknacre

This Is Me

I will draw something for you,
Perhaps then, I don't know what to do,
I want to be a medic when I'm older,
I hope no one will get hurt on the shoulder,
I like to play video games,
I like to play Roblox
All the games are the same.

Nathan Meier (10)
Priory Primary School, Bicknacre

How You Make Me

One Switch,
A sprinkle of Minecraft,
Five Among Us,
Half of YouTube,
Luigi and Mario,
A Harvey,
Two PCs,
A teaspoon of family,
Put it in a bowl and mix,
Put it in the oven for one hour,
Take it out,
And voila!

Fletcher Barnard (8)
Priory Primary School, Bicknacre

This Is Me

T eacher is nice
H orses are nice and beautiful
I am funny
S illy billy

I love my family
S ong to sing

M y family are amazing
E at food like chocolate (of course).

Lacey Cooper (8)
Priory Primary School, Bicknacre

My Life Story

Love koalas,
They make a noise, *ooh-la-la*,
Eeek! I adore hashbrowns,
I'll just sit on the sofa,
I'm watching TV,
My favourite is DVG Fam,
It's the best,
And I love solving quests,
This is me.

Isla Hone (9)
Priory Primary School, Bicknacre

All The Things I Like

I like to splash around in cold water,
I like to eat a brown, soft mixture,
I like to play matches on a Sunday morning, without using my feet,
I like to have a big bunch of people,
I like to have a water animal that you can keep as a pet.

Emily Jones (10)
Priory Primary School, Bicknacre

Roblox Is The Best

R oblox is my thing
O nce a day is enough for me
B oys mostly
L earn how to play Roblox
O nce I've played longer, I will have Robux to get skins and styles
X box, you can't play Roblox on.

Ethan Jones (7)
Priory Primary School, Bicknacre

The Dogs And Me

Me and my dogs are super silly,
And they don't let me stroke them,
But they lick me so much,
And they sometimes tread on my foot,
They sometimes are scared of me,
My dogs get worried when the doorbell rings.

Thomas Napier (8)
Priory Primary School, Bicknacre

Great Recipe

You will need a dash of kindness,
A pinch of helpfulness,
A bit of sportiness,
A large amount of healthiness,
A bit of animal-ness,
A bit of train-ness,
A bit of Tottenham-ness,
This is me.

Benjamin Linton (7)
Priory Primary School, Bicknacre

Me

S teven is my name
T o play Fortnite's my favourite game
E verything is fun
V ery fun indeed
E lephants are cool
N othing is better than my friends and family.

Steven Fell (9)
Priory Primary School, Bicknacre

Amazing Active Me

Jumping and running,
Wind is blowing,
Playing football when it's snowing,
Smell the chlorine,
Hear the echoes and splashes too,
Running as fast as a cheetah,
Winning lots of races.

Jenson King
Priory Primary School, Bicknacre

I Love My Kitten

You are the best,
I am here for you,
I will look after you,
You are okay little kitten,
Little kitten, don't be afraid,
I love you very much little kitten.
Love from Isla.

Isla Davis (7)
Priory Primary School, Bicknacre

That's Me

Lovely Lola,
Curious George,
Two lovely dogs,
Me and my grandparents,
My cousins too,
Got ice cream, it was fun,
Me and my parents,
Got a new lorry this year.

Senn-Rico Lawrenson (9)
Priory Primary School, Bicknacre

All About Me

A kennings poem.

I am a...
Online viewer,
Football seeker,
Food eater,
Rugby observer,
Game knower,
YouTube watcher,
PS4 player,
Dog lover,
Gorilla liker.

Henry Whitehead (9)
Priory Primary School, Bicknacre

Me

P oppy is my name
O n and off my tablet goes
P opping sweets into my mouth
P izza is my favourite food
Y ummy gummies in my mouth.

Poppy Jehan (9)
Priory Primary School, Bicknacre

This Is Me

A kennings poem

Book reader,
Day modeller,
Pizza eater,
Lego builder,
Music maker,
Toy lover,
Early riser,
Bike rider,
This is me.

Esme Playle (9)
Priory Primary School, Bicknacre

Fidget Person

A kennings poem

I'm a,
Dimple popper,
Football player,
YouTube watcher,
Roblox avatar,
Dog owner,
Gymnastics lover,
This is me.

Philippa Sheriff (9)
Priory Primary School, Bicknacre

Harley

A pinch of bouncy,
A handful of friendliness,
A dash of clumsy,
A spoonful of happiness,
This is me.

Harley Webb (7)
Priory Primary School, Bicknacre

This Is Me

You will need:
3 tablespoons of craziness
A dash of silliness
10g of fun
Sprinkle of kindness

How to bake:
Firstly, you will need to create the base.
All you need is craziness, silly sugar and fun.
Now to get started.
First, add in a big bowl some silly sugar and cool flour and mix gently.
Then add three happy chippy eggs and keep stirring.
Add 10g of fun and keep stirring.
Then add 3 tablespoons of craziness
Put on a tiny tray and bake for 30 minutes.
Take it out and decorate with some delicious icing

Oh wow! It's me!

Eva Pierson (10)
St Swithun Wells Catholic Primary School, Hunters Hill

This Is Me

Movies and shows are the best
Sitting by a fire there's no contest
Dark red and baby blue
Video games are great like Pac-Man, Mario and FIFA 22
There's no better subject than history
I love music listening to Magic, Heart and Kisstory
I adore Domino's and love cookies
To playing football I'm no rookie
Winter is great with hot cocoa
If you don't like London or Paris, you're loco
Hanging with my friends is what I love
Disneyland is amazing with rides 300 metres above
Fulham is my football team and the place I loved to be
When it comes to favourite drinks mines Tea
A great place is Spain
If you don't like David Walliams you're lame
Ireland is the best
Dogs are cool leave the rest
I love lying down in blankets galore

Strawberries are amazing screaming more
Learning is what I love to do
This is me. How about you?

Henry Oliver
St Swithun Wells Catholic Primary School, Hunters Hill

This Is Me

You will need:
A splash of unique
50g of books
500ml of art
A large glass of happiness
A pinch of blue
A tsp of dogs
A tbs of rabbits

How to bake:
1. Firstly, get your bowl which should be as big as an elephant
2. Next, add your happiness, books and art and whisk for 10 minutes whilst slowly pouring in the unique.
3. After that, add your dogs, rabbits and blue and mix with a spoon until true.
4. Finally, put in the oven until a peachy colour.

And that's how you make...
Me.

Maya
St Swithun Wells Catholic Primary School, Hunters Hill

This Is Me

Hello I'm Alicja
It's really nice to see ya
I really like netball
But not a fan of football
I love drawing
Even when it's pouring
I adore purple and pink
While drinking a delicious drink
I love writing to my friends
With all my new perfect pens
I love my droopy dog
And I also like slimy frogs
My favourite thing to do is watch Netflix
While munching on my tasty breadsticks
I love playing Roblox
Even in my fluffy socks
What's that I see
Oh yeah this is me.

Alicja Pszenna (10)
St Swithun Wells Catholic Primary School, Hunters Hill

This Is Me

T his is me
H er or he, they will still be my friend
I can run, I can jump, I swim and bake
S chool is my hobby

I like cats as cute as a koala
S ee the sea I like the waves when they go *whoosh*

M e and you look different
E ight takeaway five that's how many siblings I have

U rsula is my actual name
L asagne is the food that I really like
A frica feels like a calm place to be.

Ula Kumorowska (9)
St Swithun Wells Catholic Primary School, Hunters Hill

This Is Me

T he colour beautiful blue is my favourite because it is shiny like
A ncient, expensive crystal. I like playing ping pong because when I play, I am like a soft, crazy octopus
D oodling makes me as calm as a tiny, red ladybird flying around the room
H ave a good day like me on fantastic Christmas Day
G eography is one of my favourite subjects because I really like globes and when I spin a massive globe, I can hear it screaming quietly, *crash*.

Tadhg Gorman (10)
St Swithun Wells Catholic Primary School, Hunters Hill

This Is Me

M y swimming skills are very good - as good as a whale. *Splash! Splash! Splash!*
I am very kind to my family, and I will be for one million years.
K indness to my family and friends, my cat. I am as friendly as a dog and as kind as a bunny.
O nly I can be as kind as a teddy bear.
L ove is my superpower; I love sports and I love my cat.
A ll water sports I love the same.
J ogging and warmups are good for me.

Mikolaj Borowski (9)
St Swithun Wells Catholic Primary School, Hunters Hill

This Is Me

Swimming is my favourite sport
Winning is the best especially gold
I'm always tired after swimming for an hour or so
My name is Eirene by the way
My friends are kind and funny
Lois, Caitlin, Maya and Julia are my friends
No one says I'm slow, they say I'm fast
I'm always at the front of the lane
Going really fast on breaststroke
My time is 1 min 40 seconds for four lengths
in other words 100 meters in one go.

Eirene Alexaki (10)
St Swithun Wells Catholic Primary School, Hunters Hill

This Is Me

I love magical, majestic chess
I like making mess
I love charming chameleons that are as scaly as a fish
I love wizards that can grant you a magical wish
I love blue, it feels like you're in the blue Mariana Trench
I love fancy books that can wrench
I love cricket when I hit the ball *whoosh!* It goes higher than space
I love gorillas, they're part of the apes.
Bang! What is that? This is me!

Aidan Mathew (9)
St Swithun Wells Catholic Primary School, Hunters Hill

This Is Me

V is for Veronika and this poem is about me
E ven or odd I don't mind
R ain is pouring down and I don't like it
O n my birthday I wish for a dog as soft as clouds
N otes on the keyboard are easy to play
I n my heart I keep magenta and blue
K ind friend I am and full of happiness
A nd this is the end of my poem and now you know me more!

Veronika Vlasakova
St Swithun Wells Catholic Primary School, Hunters Hill

This Is Me

To play football I'm a pro
I'm a goalie diving high and low
My favourite player, Kai Havertz, he's the best
No player can contest
I'm a sports guy running along
The sensation of taking shin pads off I long
Making a save gives a smile to my face
Before I put on my trusty boots and do my lace
We won, we are so great
After the match we celebrate.

Matas
St Swithun Wells Catholic Primary School, Hunters Hill

This Is Me

I love PE
And I love to learn
Flowers make me smile
When I lay them on the tile
I love ballet in my bright pink tutu
I adore dancing too
I love drawing
Even when it's pouring
I love the colour red
And I also love tasty bread
I have two brothers
And I love basketball
The ball starts to scream at me when I pass it
This is me.

Scarlett Gibaut (9)
St Swithun Wells Catholic Primary School, Hunters Hill

This Is Me

Blake is my name
I like doing experiments with no blame
Always going to be me
Kind, I'm always trusting to be
Every day I smile
The dinosaurs haven't existed for a while
Happy as a hippogriff
On the side of an enormous cliff
Mean is not my way
Poems... hip hip hooray
Snakes are the best

This is me!

Blake
St Swithun Wells Catholic Primary School, Hunters Hill

This Is Me

F un, funny goofy me
R unning in the snow because it's as fluffy as a cloud
A s fun as a Christmas day
N etball is my favourite sport
C ats are as cute as dogs
E ating cheesy pizzas
S lapping my tea as quick as I can
C aring like a deer
A lways talking for one million years.

Francesca Ma (9)
St Swithun Wells Catholic Primary School, Hunters Hill

This Is Me

A ll water sports I really like
G reat flippers are from Nike
A ching legs wandering around
T all people kicking hard
A rms flying like a card.

S the word begins with
K its from the company Liv
I ce-cold water
B e a wonderful daughter
A ll people are allowed.

Agata Skiba
St Swithun Wells Catholic Primary School, Hunters Hill

This Is Me

L uciana is me mostly happy me
U nique eyes popping out as bright as a fire
C hatting as loud as a lion roaring
I am as happy as a person meeting a dog
A person who is funky and fun
N etball is my favourite sport
I t screams when I throw it.
A person who loves roaming around.

Luciana

St Swithun Wells Catholic Primary School, Hunters Hill

This Is Me

A kennings poem

I am a...
Football player
An early riser
A good helper
A kind person
McDonald's eater
A gamer
A caring person
A late sleeper
A small person
And finally, a fun person.

Mark Novetsky (9)
St Swithun Wells Catholic Primary School, Hunters Hill

This Is Me

For this recipe you will need:
10 drops of fancy fashion
8 sprinkles of silly silliness
5 magic tablespoons of matureness
100g of kindness
And *boom!*
You have made me.

Evie Kilgannon (9)
St Swithun Wells Catholic Primary School, Hunters Hill

This Is Me

Fluffy and scruffy
As cute as a teddy bear
Very silly but extra loud
Ball of fluff
Tiny and adorable
As messy as a bog
Happy and playful
What's my favourite animal?

Lilliana Ryder (9)
St Swithun Wells Catholic Primary School, Hunters Hill

This Is Me

A kennings poem

I am a...
Fancy footballer
Swimming winner
Majestic mathematician
Silly salmon
Power player
Funny friend
Terrifying trampoliner
Cute koala lover
This is me!

Henry Lane
St Swithun Wells Catholic Primary School, Hunters Hill

This Is Me

A kennings poem

I am a...
Chocolate eater
Gamer
Food lover
Bad joker
Movie fun
Werewolves fan
McDonald's lover
Cat hater
Dog lover
This is me.

Jake Flanagan (10)
St Swithun Wells Catholic Primary School, Hunters Hill

This Is Me

Cats are the best.
They purr like the wind.
Their whiskers are like long pieces
of grass on the hills.
They rest their furry heads on the ground
and sleep.

Ava Hillier (10)
St Swithun Wells Catholic Primary School, Hunters Hill

Nucleus

I am the clear, sweet voice of a bird,
I am the soul of the gentlest waterfall,
I am a curious, smart mind, whose vigour has no end,
I am the sturdy, robust force in a fist,
I am the true, pure freedom that everyone desires,
I am the darkest of blacks, more powerful than the rest,
I am the fearless, red passion that burns in a heart,
I am the endlessly working ant who never stops,
I am the tumultuous, turbulent ocean that rages with unrest,
Nobody should hide their profound hidden side,
Because of their pride,
I don't want to conceal the way I feel.

Jahnel Marseglia-Mendy (10)
St Vincent De Paul RC Primary School, London

This Is My Life

T hank you for my family and for my friendship
H aving jokes with my friends
I n London where I stay
S taying at home, my favourite place

I like playing football with my brother
S t Vincent is the best school I've ever been to

M y favourite sibling is my big brother and my little sister
Y ear 2021 has been the best year for me

L ike playing games with everyone in my class
I want to spend time with my family
F inding stuff when it is lost
E ating pizza, my favourite food.

Thomas Nyakuchena (10)
St Vincent De Paul RC Primary School, London

Fantasy

I can be
Anything in my fantasy,
From a teacher to a vet,
I can let
My imagination fly,
As I zoom across the sky,
But as the birds sing,
My alarm clock pings,
I wake up and *boom!*
I'm back in my room,
But I close my eyes,
The dawn-light dies,
And I'm back where I can be,
Anything I want to be,
Here inside my fantasy,
From a bear to a bee,
An angel to an aardvark,
Or a woodpecker eating bark,
But dreams come true,
For me and you,

Your imagination will never leave,
If only you believe!

Elizabeth Fothergill (11)
St Vincent De Paul RC Primary School, London

Alonso Is Me

My name is Alonso,
Mum named me after a race car driver,
But no thanks, I prefer to be a good goalkeeper,
More like a climber, high in the air,
I'm live, sky-high sweeper,
Going to school I always keep it cool,
Unlike my big brother, who is always acting like a fool,
My mum, she's from South Africa, they call it the Motherland,
I love my family but of the food, I'm not always a fan,
I love knowing all this history,
But knowing what I love is no mystery,
England is the land in my heart,
And no matter where I go, we will never be apart.

Alonso Landers (10)
St Vincent De Paul RC Primary School, London

This Is Me

A music lover who loves dancing to Jason Derulo,
A shopping lover who loves to buy clothes (and doesn't care about the cost sometimes),
A book lover who loves to read Diary of a Wimpy Kid,
A cheese lover who loves to eat cheese (except blue cheese),
This is me,
I love making food and cakes,
I love myself and I am unique,
I love watching Life Stories by this man called Dhar Mann,
I love everyone and I am honest,
I love one song called 'Love Not War' by Jason Derulo,
I am Sophia and I love me.

Sophia Oamhen (9)
St Vincent De Paul RC Primary School, London

This Is Me

T hankful that I have the talent of running
H onest and I try my hardest at all times
I love my family and friends because they always support me
S inging really lifts my mood when I feel like giving up

I can always rely on my siblings even though they're annoying
S pending all my time practising my running

M aking an effort every day with my running can really help
E qual or not, I will always be a special and talented person.

Chayse Pryce (10)
St Vincent De Paul RC Primary School, London

This Is Me

T rying to make friendships and help others
H aving time to spend with my family and friends
I n a kind world to be in
S wimming is what I do on Fridays and Tuesdays

I am thankful and loving to everybody
S t Vincent De Paul is the best school for me

M y teachers, family, friends, and more to love
E ven though my brothers annoy me a lot, even
when I am doing something important, I love
them as much as I love myself.

Lena Maria Dabrowska (10)

St Vincent De Paul RC Primary School, London

Which Direction

Which direction should I go?
Left, right, up, or down?
When I get lost in a test, which direction should I go?
When I am being mistreated, which direction should I go?
When someone betrays me, which direction should I go?
When I can't avoid danger, which direction should I go?
If I don't know which direction is best,
Then I cannot travel by myself,
But I know that
There will always be someone to guide me,
For the first time.

Brandon Greg Cuntapay (10)
St Vincent De Paul RC Primary School, London

This Is My World

This is me, no apologies,
I am happy to be me,
This is me, no apologies,
I wouldn't change for you to be pleased,
This is me, no apologies,
My world is a canvas with bright colours like me,
This is me, no apologies,
I'm happy to be with my family,
This is me, no apologies,
I love sports and being last isn't an option,
This is me, no apologies,
I build my world, brick by brick,
This is me.

Elsa Quainoo (9)
St Vincent De Paul RC Primary School, London

Who Are You?

I am a vicious tiger, waiting to feed on prey,
I am a venomous fly-trap, waiting for a fly to step into my trap,
I am Iron Man saving the world from a purple alien who is trying to make half of the world vanish,
I am a tiny ant, roaming places without being seen,
I am a black colour that represents how powerful I am,
I am a comfy chair, waiting for someone to sit on me,
Everything I am, I'm still always optimistic.

Aiden J Reyes Abella (10)
St Vincent De Paul RC Primary School, London

My Life

T he best food in the world is noodles
H ot sometimes but very tasty
I absolutely love art and I want to be an architect
S ometimes I sketch portraits when I am bored

I think that dancing is the best sport ever
S o my family always cheers me on

M y birds always go bonkers, but I still love them
E ating, dancing, family, art, and my birds are my life!

Radha-Rupa Burke (9)
St Vincent De Paul RC Primary School, London

This Is Me

T hankful for my life
H aving a game of football can change my mood
I speak English and Polish
S itting with my family and watching a film I love

I was born in London and currently live there
S t Vincent De Paul is where I go to school

M y family is what I love from my heart
E ven though we get into arguments.

Jakub Borek (10)
St Vincent De Paul RC Primary School, London

A Day In My Life

A kennings poem

I am a...
Family lover,
Brilliant game player,
Good football player,
Book reader,
Judge becomer,
JoJo's Bizarre Adventure watcher,
Amazing maths lover,
Food lover,
School goer,
Dragon lover,
Friend lover,
Fantastic Nerf Gun player,
Music listener,
English lover,
History lover,
Movie watcher,
And finally, a believer.

Sam Farella (10)
St Vincent De Paul RC Primary School, London

This Is Me

T rying hard at school is my thing
H appiness, weirdness and being thoughtful
I ndependence on a bike
S ister and cousin, Francine

I s tranquilness my thing?
S adness isn't really my thing

M um, Dad, Jesus, is home with me
E legance at church, singing and dancing with
weirdness is my thing.

Aliyah Marie Coopera (9)
St Vincent De Paul RC Primary School, London

This Is Me

T hankful for my friends
H aving a great big laugh with friends
I s the best thing that can ever happen
S miling is my favourite

I play with my friends
S chool is the place for friendship

M y family and friends are my favourite things
E ven though we do argue, we all love each other.

Luca Takahashi (9)
St Vincent De Paul RC Primary School, London

Recipe To Make Me

What you need:
A book,
A brilliant younger brother,
A family of laughter,
A circus of my own,
Ten pizzas,
And a bag of sugar.

Now, where to start,
First the pizza and sugar,
Next family of laughter and circus of my own,
Don't forget an amazing younger brother,
And a storybook,
You've made me!

Grace Winters (10)
St Vincent De Paul RC Primary School, London

Having Fun

I am a loving family member,
I am a funny friend,
I am a pupil at St Vincent De Paul,
I am a Nerf Gun battler,
I am an animal lover,
I am a Rocket League Champion,
I am a Minecraft Pro,
I am a football player,
I am a music listener,
I am a school lover,
I am a margarita pizza lover,
Finally, I am a dragon lover!

Noah Agustin (9)
St Vincent De Paul RC Primary School, London

I Am Everything

I am a creepy crocodile crawling,
A fine flower blooming in spring,
I am everything,
I am Willy Wonka who loves sweets,
A leaf floating in the whooshing wind,
I am everything,
I am red, glowing with rage,
A chair waiting to be sat on,
I am everything,
I am bold, not frightened and fierce,
I am everything.

John Jabbour
St Vincent De Paul RC Primary School, London

Welcome To My World

This is me,
A young little sister,
Very dramatic with a pinch of who looks picture-perfect,
With a little dog called Tyson,
I have two older brothers,
I am a kind and caring person,
I love playing with my friends and brothers,
My dog is my best friend,
My favourite game is hide-and-seek,
And this is my world.

Megan Trujillo Castano (9)
St Vincent De Paul RC Primary School, London

The Happy Nugget

I am a brave bird soaring through the air,
I am a beautiful rose, ready to grow,
I am a 'Where's Wally?' hiding among the crowd,
I am a small sticker ready to be used,
I am the colour yellow like the bright sun,
I am a divine couch ready to be sat on,
I am happy because I think on the bright side.

Genesis Yunda (10)
St Vincent De Paul RC Primary School, London

A Lion Roaming

I am a lively lion cub that loves to play at dawn,
I am the wild sea, rushing with ideas,
I am Percy Jackson with astounding strength,
I am a needle in a haystack,
I am light blue, light red, and light yellow combined,
I am a blanket, ready to wrap up,
I am quiet, passionate, adventurous and happy.

Maria Sandoval (10)

St Vincent De Paul RC Primary School, London

I Am

I am a sleepy sloth snoring,
I am a flower waiting to die,
I am Podkin, waiting to take my enemies down one by one,
I am a tiny seed waiting to grow,
I am chairs piled on top of each other, supported by each other,
I am anger waiting to be unleashed,
This is me.

Lucas Gorka Bond (10)
St Vincent De Paul RC Primary School, London

I Am A...

A kennings poem

Custard cream eater,
Good illustrator,
Great reader,
Amazing friend,
Funny classmate,
Kind-hearted helper,
Happy,
Amazing handwriter,
Fabulous dancer,
Learning Halo,
And finally, artistic creator.

Phoenix-Halo Mokonen Agyemang (10)
St Vincent De Paul RC Primary School, London

If I Were.....

If I were a soup, I'd be every single colour,
Mixed up in my own unique pattern,
Add a dollop of friendship,
Pour in some care,
Then add some cheek,
And some laughter to share.

If I were a soup, I'd taste sweet with a kick,
I wouldn't be thin but I wouldn't be thick,
A pattern that is one of a kind,
A thousand different colours that have all been combined.

If I were a cookie, I'd be fresh out the oven,
Gooey with a bit of a crunch,
Milk chocolate chips melted inside,
Each one bursting with kindness.

If I were a cookie, I'd be rough around the edges,
I wouldn't be perfectly formed,
For no one and nothing can ever be perfect,
No one recipe fits all.

Rosie Whiting (10)
Wiveliscombe Primary School, Wiveliscombe

YoungWriters Est. 1991

YOUNG WRITERS INFORMATION

We hope you have enjoyed reading this book – and that you will continue to in the coming years.

If you're the parent or family member of an enthusiastic poet or story writer, do visit our website **www.youngwriters.co.uk/subscribe** and sign up to receive news, competitions, writing challenges and tips, activities and much, much more! There's lots to keep budding writers motivated!

If you would like to order further copies of this book, or any of our other titles, then please give us a call or order via your online account.

Young Writers
Remus House
Coltsfoot Drive
Peterborough
PE2 9BF
(01733) 890066
info@youngwriters.co.uk

Join in the conversation!
Tips, news, giveaways and much more!

YoungWritersUK YoungWritersCW youngwriterscw